ST ANDREW'S

THE STORY OF A BOOKSHOP

1957-1997

Sandra Carter

St Andrew's Bookshop Ltd

Illustration of Great Missenden High Street on front of
jacket by Barry Dow; coloured by Edwina Hannam

Designed by Peter Wyart, Three's Company

Produced by
Angus Hudson Ltd,
Concorde House, Grenville Place,
Mill Hill, London NW7 3SA, England
Tel: +44 181 959 3668
Fax +44 181 959 3678

Printed in Singapore

ST ANDREW'S

THE STORY OF A BOOKSHOP

1957-1997

Sandra Carter

Mrs Zettie Clark outside 65 High Street,
Great Missenden, about 1957.

CONTENTS

1. Small Beginnings — 11

2. Out of the Ashes . . . — 17

3. Reaching out — 24

4. Expansion — 30

5. Paper Pastors and Book Agents — 45

6. What's the Point of Books? — 48

7. I'd like to run a Christian bookshop . . . — 55

8. Is the Book Finished? — 57

Twelve Significant Books — 60

FOREWORD

We often liken the story of St Andrew's Bookshops to the parable of the mustard seed.

It began 40 years ago, with one lady sharing with another her vision to see the Christian faith spread through Christian literature. Over the past 40 years it has grown, almost like a family tree, involving many people in its ministry, both staff and customers.

Many of these customers have become faithful Book Agents, taking our resources into the local churches; and our supporters' financial help over the years has enabled our ministry to grow.

To each and every one of you we would like to say a big thank you. To Mrs Zettie Clark for listening to God's promptings. To Sandra Carter for her gift in collating all our thoughts and putting them into some order. To our friends at Angus Hudson Ltd and Three's Company for sharing in our vision and making the printing of this book possible.

Thank you to our Lord, for making it ALL possible, directing our paths and not letting us stand still. The seed is still growing and by the time this book is published a new work of St Andrew's will have started in Wokingham, not in the High Street but in a craft village at Holme Grange – another story. *To God be the glory.*

Ernie and Margaret Barnett

Inside St Andrew's bookshop, Great Missenden.

Chapter 1
Small Beginnings

It all began with corn plasters and bunion pads.

In 1957 Zettie Clark leafed through the pages of a magazine as she waited to see the chiropodist, Doris Wall, at 63, High Street, Great Missenden.

Zettie Clark noticed that passers-by often looked at the chiropody sales table in the window or popped in to make an enquiry. A thought struck her: If really worthwhile books were displayed here – Christian books and specially the Bible – perhaps people might stop to look and buy, and meet the Saviour of whom they spoke.

The stirrings of an idea. She could hardly have imagined that today, 40 years later, that chiropodist's room in a quiet Buckinghamshire village would have become a thriving Christian bookshop with seven branches serving three counties.

Zettie Clark's previous attempts to introduce Christian books in the village – a small shelf of booklets at the back of the local Baptist church – had met a conspicuous lack of response. She thought herself lucky if she found more than 3d in the money box each week.

She shared her vision for a small table of books in the chiropodist's waiting-room with Doris Wall, who had recently become a Christian, and she treasured for years the letter the foot specialist wrote in response. It seems Miss Wall already had a glimpse of what the Holy Spirit might do with their willingness to be used in his service in this small way:

'I have given much thought to "our little shop". Do

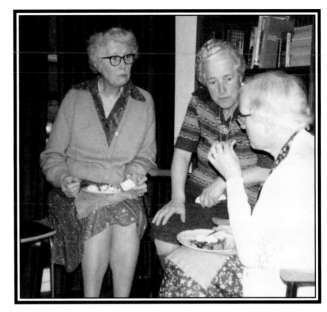

Left to right: Mrs Leila Davy, sister of Zettie Clark, Miss Doris Wall, chiropodist, and Mrs Zettie Clark, founder.

you think that will be our way of "selling Christ" to others? It occurs to me that the seller (myself) might best qualify as a buyer! However, as suggested, I am trying to lie still in this matter and wait for his guidance.

'Our little shop lies dormant. For years it has lain unlit, unfulfilled. Like myself, of no definite purpose – just existing . . .

'Then on 25 November we heard a sermon on St Andrew – the introducer – and we thrilled at the thought of being used as introducers in this village, and next day you wrote, "The little shop shall serve him, and we shall set up yet another St Andrew in this village to which he has directed us."'

The adventure had begun. They placed the first order for £10 worth of Bibles and books as a book agency with the Christian Literature Crusade, set them out on a table in the chiropodist's waiting room, and St Andrew's bookshop was born.

The date was 12 March, 1957. The first sale was a

The chiropodist's shop with Christian books on display in the window.

could flourish in so small a village – the population of Great Missenden is only some 6,000. Perhaps people prefer to drive through the lanes of 'leafy Bucks' for books rather than make a trip to London. And unlike some shopping centres it is hard to get lost in the village. It has only one main street and parking nearby is easy.

From the beginning, a large Bible was placed in the shop window with a different page open each day and a light illuminating it till late at night – a feature that continued for many years. Often when people came out of the pub opposite at night, they would cross the road and look in to read the open Bible. A passer-by wrote saying, 'After a period of overstrain and a short holiday to get over it, your Bible in the window open at Psalm 112 was simply a God-given word in season for a family man going back to his responsibilities.'

Bible and the first month's takings were £13 19s 61/2d. From that small but faithful start, the annual turnover for St Andrew's and its seven branches in Buckinghamshire, Berkshire and Oxfordshire is now around £1.3m.

It was not long before the Bibles and books found a more prominent place. Out went the corn plasters and bunion pads from the shop's large display window. In went the books.

But not even that was good enough for the chiropodist. She announced: 'God now has my life – he shall have the shop as well!' Her practice moved to the back room and the shop and window were given over to Christian books.

As interest grew and stocks increased, the shop was soon bursting at the seams. News was spreading that Christian literature was available in Great Missenden and customers began coming from as far away as Slough, Maidenhead and Watford.

It might seem strange that a specialised bookshop

From barbers to Bibles

The following year, 1958, the barber's shop next door became vacant. It was up for sale at a very reasonable £1,500, but no buyers came forward. Zettie Clark began to think, 'Perhaps God is keeping that shop for us.' It was purchased and the crowded little shop was able to expand through a newly cut archway in the 18-inch-thick dividing wall.

How many heads had been trimmed or chins shaved in the 100 years of the barber's shop's life was beyond computing. But there was evidence enough under the lino. Zettie Clark shuddered to recall the cleaning-up of the inch-thick layer of hair clippings buried there.

Despite its growth and success, Zettie Clark never saw the bookshop as a business. It was a mission – a way of winning people for Christ and building up the faith of Christians. She subsidised the operation for 14 years, often doing the books late at night and ploughing all the profits back in. It was a busy venture since she also supported her husband in his business and local government activities, cared for six children, and spoke frequently at women's meetings.

The barber's shop next door became an extension to the shop in 1958.

Words of power

The bookshop was meeting a need. Letters arrived from many who had been helped by the literature they bought there, or from the quiet witness of Zettie Clark herself.

One customer wrote from Sidmouth, Devon, in 1961: 'You will be surprised to receive this letter, but I feel I would like to thank you for the great help you gave to me, when some two years ago I chanced to call in your shop to make an enquiry about the new edition of the English Bible.

'At the time I was extremely anxious about my husband's health but after a talk with you both, I came away much relieved and the little book you suggested proved to be a wonderful help. I feel I cannot thank you enough for your kindness and help.

'My faith at that time was very weak; but you gave me fresh hope and I was able to carry on. I feel sure I was led to your shop that day, and I have always wished to tell you what great comfort and help you gave to me.

'I didn't pay quite the full price for this book. I know you let me have it cheaper than the real price. At the time I couldn't think clearly. Please accept the enclosed stamps.'

The 'upper room' was part of St Andrew's in the early days, a room set out as a chapel where anyone could go to pray, or where troubles could be shared and prayed over.

Through the back of the shop a door led to a quite different kind of room – a noisy room with a big box of toys, where children could play while their parents browsed among the books ('particularly useful for ministers with large families!').

Moving on

The bookshop continued to thrive under the partnership of Zettie Clark and Doris Wall until 1966. Then the chiropodist moved to another district. New helpers were needed. It had been a fruitful nine-year co-operation, but who was available to help now?

Just at this time the prospect was looking gloomy for Geoff Davy, Zettie Clark's brother-in-law. He had to retire early from his job after a bout of heart trouble, but felt fit enough to cope with a less demanding job. It was soon clear that this apparent calamity, as so often in the Christian life, was going to 'work together for good'. The top floor over the two shops was converted into a flat and Geoff and his wife Leila moved in with their two children. The need was met perfectly.

Geoff later recalled, 'Leila had always wanted a house with character and now she got it, for the shops date from 1642, the time of Charles I, and old wooden beams have been uncovered in the shop and two upstairs rooms. Under the floor in what was then the sitting room and is now part of the shop is a well, for this part of the building was built over the old courtyard, and outside is a pump which used to supply several properties round about.'

One notable visitor during this time was Harold Wilson, who, while Prime Minister, called in for Christmas cards on his way to Chequers.

With this couple, as with Zettie Clark, the work was done in response to the call of God and as a means of spreading the good news of Jesus Christ, their only financial remuneration being rent-free accommodation. They continued to help until Geoff's health deteriorated in 1973. Geoff died in 1980, but Leila still lives above the shop.

Besides being a normal retail outlet, St Andrew's Bookshop always tried to go a step further in encouraging wider use of Christian books. In the early days there was concern for the local Polish population, former wartime refugees. Polish Scriptures were always on display in the chiropodist's waiting room, the customer often being engaged in conversation about its message as toes were treated.

Book agencies were an important feature of the outreach of the shop early on too. By 1972 agencies were running in more than 50 churches and homes in the area, and the figure had doubled by 1978.

It became clear that Zettie Clark and her sister could no longer continue running the shop, with Geoff now unable to help. So in 1973 they began to make enquiries in the Christian book trade and missionary societies in the hope that someone would be found to take over the shop, if possible running it on similar lines as before.

For a while there was little response. But God had two people ready to take charge of the shop. In fact he had been preparing them for this moment for some years.

The bookshop was run from one desk in the early days. Margaret and Ernie with Tim – and the cat.

Prepared for the job

Ernie Barnett had begun his working life in an accounts office. Itchy feet and a desire to spread the gospel took him to Concordia, a film distributor and book publisher, as a sales representative. He was well known at the shop both as a local book agent and as Concordia rep. Ernie's wife Margaret had been the secretary to Concordia's British manager before their children came along, so she too had some knowledge of the Christian book trade. Ernie was also well known in the area as a local preacher.

Knowing that St Andrew's needed a manager, Ernie casually tossed out the suggestion to David Alexander that St Andrew's Bookroom would make a good base and distribution centre for his new venture, Lion Publishing; and that he, Ernie, would be quite happy to manage the shop for him.

To Ernie's great surprise the suggestion was taken up. In September 1973 he found himself working at St Andrew's despatching the new Lion titles and in the following January took over the management of the shop and distribution centre.

Ernie Barnett remembers those four years of Lion ownership as 'exciting, eventful and hardworking'. The retail business continued to grow, while the wooden shed in the back yard became a hive of activity as Lion Publishing leapt to the forefront of the Christian book scene. It was at this time that *The Lion Handbook to the Bible* was published. Orders poured in from all over the world, and tens of thousands of books were despatched from the little back shed.

Ernie and Margaret remember discovering that even the mechanics of a distribution system can be committed to the Lord and his help found. For instance, space was at a premium as trade increased, and on more than one occasion the staff had just cleared a space in the packed shed when an unexpected delivery of some thousand or more books arrived, which might have caused utter chaos.

Lion had owned the business for four years when on a car journey from Oxford David Alexander casually asked Ernie, 'Would you be interested in buying the bookshop?'

Of course he would – it had long been Ernie and Margaret's dream to own a bookshop. But with only £75 in savings between them what could they do?

An accountant friend, Peter Smails, suggested they buy the business over a period of time. Lion agreed, providing the Barnetts could find a down-payment of £3,000. The Barnetts and their friends began to pray.

The bank promised £2,000 if the would-be shop owners could find the remaining £1,000. They were still short to the tune of an elusive £925.

But by the morning after the visit to the bank, the whole picture had dramatically changed. By that time Christian friends had rallied round offering to lend £4,500. The bank offer was no longer required. They had more cash in hand than Lion had asked for, and the way ahead was open.

On Saturday 1st April, 1977, 60 friends of St Andrew's Bookshop met for a Service of Dedication led by John Perry, who is now Bishop of Chelmsford. Ownership of the business was formally handed over to Ernie and Margaret Barnett. Zettie Clark, who still owned the property, was delighted. So were the Davys. They knew just how much the Barnetts valued Christian books, and how committed they were to the spiritual ministry of the bookshop. St Andrew's was in good hands.

It was much more than a business transaction. And, as is so often the case, God had used the whole process of decision-making and the search for finance to test and strengthen the faith of the shop's new owners.

Ernie says, 'There was a time when we greatly desired a bookshop of our own, but while working at St Andrew's in the early days as its manager, this desire completely went. I have learnt a great lesson here. Often when we lose the desire for something, God gives it to us – to use it for him.'

But even when the offer of the bookshop had been made and the down-payment found, the final decision still was not easy. There was still £13,000 of stock to be paid off over a three-year period. But Ernie said, 'We felt God had opened the door and we needed to step through in faith.'

They did. Under their management and later proprietorship, the shop continued its growth. It became the hub of an energetic, cheerful, friendly and effective ministry.

Zettie Clark subsequently arranged for St Andrew's Bookshop Ltd to buy the premises at a favourable price, with the proviso that Leila could continue living there.

Chapter 2
Out of the Ashes . . .

Ernie and Margaret Barnett had been proprietors of the shop for less than a year when disaster struck. In the early hours of Monday, 26th February 1978, 70-year-old Geoff Davy and his wife Leila lay asleep in their flat above the bookshop.

Across the High Street in the Red Lion, the publican's daughter Christine, like many 17-year-olds, had no desire to sleep and sat watching the late night film on TV. She made ready for bed at 1.15am.

Suddenly Christine's attention was caught by flashes of light. She looked out of the window and saw sparks coming out of the bookshop opposite. She looked closer. The left-hand corner of the building was alight.

Without hesitation she called her mother who promptly called the Fire Brigade. Meanwhile, realising that an elderly couple lived above the shop, Christine ran into the street shouting, trying to rouse Geoff and Leila Davy. Mrs Campbell came out of the Red Lion Hotel and mother and daughter ran to the back of the shop, to see if they could get the Davys' attention.

By now the inside of the shop, full of books and magazines, was beginning to burn fiercely.

Leila Davy takes up the story. 'Three sharp bangs (as the main supply cable from the electricity box blew out) wakened us. I opened the bedroom door and saw clouds of smoke coming up the stairs. Geoff phoned the fire brigade, while I went to find a way out. Picking up a very surprised cat in passing, I went down the back stairs and threw him out of the office door.'

At this point the Davys lost contact with each other

for a few worrying moments. Leila thought her husband was following her, but he had made his way down the main stairs into the shop itself. To their great relief, they met up at the back door of the shop, where they were met by an anxious Mrs Campbell, who was still trying to make them hear. She took the couple across to the Red Lion and looked after them for the rest of the night.

The local fire brigade, a part-time but efficient force, arrived in just eight minutes. Even so they did not arrive too soon. The acetate on the book jackets melted, then the chemical released built up and exploded with such force that the bookshop's heavy cash till was blown through the window. A local policeman, first official on the scene, narrowly escaped injury.

Geoff and Leila were shocked but safe, and the firemen soon had the blaze under control. But not before thousands of pounds worth of damage had been done to the shop and the stock.

The first Ernie and Margaret knew of the disaster was when police banged on the front door and woke them. They had slept through the repeated ringing of their telephone and the police had been called in. Ernie remembers, 'The officer asked did we own a bookshop in Great Missenden. We said we did and he replied, "It's burning."'

Ernie threw some clothes over his pyjamas after being assured that the Davys were safe. Then he drove the five miles of country lanes to Great Missenden 'in a state of shock', thinking perhaps the police had got the wrong bookshop.

When he arrived, the High Street was in darkness apart from the light from the pub opposite, and the lamp of a solitary fireman who emerged from the stricken shop, its windows blown out. Soon Ernie was joined by John Wearing, the husband of one of the shop's part-time staff. His wife Ruth drove out to keep Margaret company.

Ernie and John looked at the debris. Ernie recalls, 'We went into the back of that dark, damp-smelling shop. We bowed our heads in prayer and committed the future to our loving heavenly Father.'

The drama of that night still looms large in the memories of those who care about the shop.

Zettie Clark, the original owner: 'The telephone rang at 1.30am. It was a friend from the village calling. "There's a terrible fire in the High Street and it looks like St Andrew's!"

'I had five minutes to dress and get the car out. Then the never-to-be-forgotten scene of flames leaping from the ground level to upper windows.'

Ruth Wearing, one of the staff: 'The telephone woke us in the early hours of the morning. A tearful strained voice, "Ruth, the shop's on fire!" It seemed like a bad dream, but as I came to, I thought first of the Davys upstairs in the flat. Margaret said she had no details.

'My next concern was for Margaret. She was shocked and upset. John and I scrambled into our clothes. John jumped into his car to find Ernie, who was at the shop. I got into mine to go to Margaret. We sped off, our minds in a whirl, only now feeling the first horror as the reality of what was happening dawned on us.

'Margaret and I sat going over the few facts we had, just sharing the nightmare. Tim, the Barnetts' eldest son, woke. Margaret told him what had happened. I shall never forget how he sat, white-faced, a coffee cup shaking in his hand and his teeth literally chattering with shock.

'John found Ernie outside the burning shop. He seemed small and alone standing there, oblivious of the firemen and their equipment all around him. The fire was smouldering by now. They prayed for strength and courage, and that God would bring goodness out of the situation. It was all they could do.'

Ernie takes up the tale: 'Before long our minister, Wilbert Putman, arrived to offer help. Physically and practically there was little we could do. Geoff and Leila Davy went to stay with Leila's sister, Zettie Clark. John, Wilbert and I went back to our house and spent the time in prayer seeking the Lord's help and guidance.

'We were given promises from the Lord by different people, but the one that kept coming to the fore was: "Our holy and beautiful house (shop) is burned up with fire, and all our pleasant things are laid to waste . . . But O Lord, Thou art our Father"' (Isaiah 64: 11 and 8).

Good from evil

The fire seemed to be a complete tragedy. Within the year, however, everyone involved with the bookshop could see that God had wonderfully brought good out of evil.

But at the time things looked gloomy. The devastation from the fire and water was staggering, though the prompt action of the fire brigade, mostly part-timers who had reacted with incredible speed, had saved the building intact.

Ruth Wearing recalls the scene that faced them at first light. 'The things that were not burned were covered in soot or soaking wet and ruined. The rubble was ankle deep. Pictures hung crazily from the walls. Then there was the awful smell and the shocked, staring faces of the passers-by.

'I think the worst was seeing the Davys' flat so blackened, and their treasured photographs ruined. I realised how a few hours could wipe out the security of their home and bring a thriving, busy shop to an instant standstill.'

One regular book agent, unaware of what had

The building was gutted by the fire.

happened, arrived at the shop that morning. Intending to buy some books and to pass the time of day with the staff, he wept openly at the devastation of the shop, as his heart went out to Ernie and Margaret.

But tears were set aside as the grim task of clearing up and salvage began. They set to work to clear the shed for damaged but saleable stock. As they sorted through the shop, they found one remarkable escape from the damage. The Bible which had sat open as always in pride of place in the shop window was retrieved almost completely undamaged, despite fire, explosion and gallons of water. Its survival seemed symbolic. 'The Word of the Lord endures forever.'

Staff set to work with a will. Within hours, shelving was brought from another shop and erected in the shed at the back that had done such sterling service as stock room and distribution centre in Lion days. Remarkably everything seemed to fit snugly. Usable stock was put in place, and St Andrew's was in business again. Ernie immediately informed customers of the new arrangements and announced a sale, selling damaged books at bargain prices.

Response from the 'family'

Then came the first of the many blessings following the fire. Ernie and Margaret discovered how large an extended family cared for the ministry of the bookshop and for the people who ran it. Letters and cards came pouring in from church leaders, shoppers, friends, bookagents and publishers. Many sent gifts of money.

The following Sunday Ernie was due to preach at a local church. Unknown to him the congregation had collected for the bookshop, and an envelope containing £100 was put in his pocket. He got up from lunch that Sunday to find an envelope on the doormat bulging with notes, an anonymous gift.

A local Sunday school collected money. Friends set up a special fund to help replace the £17,000 worth of stock lost in the fire. It later transpired that the stock was under-insured (they were insured for the loss of stock, fixtures and fittings to the sum of around £13,000). So the donations were a lifeline in the reconstruction of the business.

One of the most moving moments came one morning when Ernie was working in the shed. A mother came in with two young children. 'They opened up their bags and gave me 30p each,' Ernie recalls. '"We want you to have this for your shop," they said. It reduced me to tears. Their mother was trying to teach them how to give and we had to learn how to receive.'

Perhaps the secret behind people's generosity was the ministry of the shop over so many years and the loving, patient service given by Ernie, Margaret and their team. Ernie had always said, 'The key is putting yourself out for people.' When he was only ten, the Barnett's youngest son Jonathan had said, with that straightforward perception of children, 'St Andrew's isn't a shop, it's a person.' The operation is people-centred. Many believe that accounts for its success over 40 years and for the support it received when it was most needed.

What a sale

Even the sale proved a blessing. It yielded £2,000 from the salvaged stock. But there was more to it than that.

Norman Burrows, then a Methodist minister locally, remembers that sale day vividly. 'What a marvellous atmosphere there was that Saturday – a wonderful feeling that the Lord was in all this. There was the usual banter with Ernie. I said here I was, first in the queue to take advantage of our friend's misfortune! Where else could this sort of thing happen except among Christians?'

Friends and contacts came from far and wide. Norman bought £66 worth of good books that day. They looked even better after his wife had, literally, ironed out the wrinkles in the pages. These were used

Margaret surveys the awful damage after the fire in 1978.

The Barnetts with Greg Thornton of Moody Press at the shed which served as a shop while fire damage was repaired.

again and again to great spiritual effect among friends and family, and in Aylesbury Prison where he was chaplain.

Ray Scorey was also at the sale. He recalls, 'I had not long become a Christian, and that day I bought my first Bible, a brown Good News version. I took it back to the home of my future father-in-law, Norman Burrows, and I remember ironing practically every page. The pages still stayed a bit crinkled so it was the noisiest Bible ever. As my first Bible it was very important to me and soon got full of underlinings in green ink.' Ray was given another Bible when he became a church member. Now a lay preacher, he keeps the Bible from the fire for use at his church.

He adds, 'What happened to that Bible is like the Christian life really. You go through the fire and get a bit smoke damaged, but God is still able to use us.'

Stock that had been out on sale or return was

received back and trips were made to wholesalers to bring in new books. The bookshop team continued to operate from the shed for nine months.

Zettie Clark had no doubt that God's hand was on the shop. 'Disaster? No! Blessing – for out of the ruins arose a new building purpose-planned for business and living – more than we had ever dreamed or hoped for! "I only design your dross to consume and your gold to refine,"' she quoted from the hymn 'How Firm a Foundation'.

A new beginning

While business ticked over in the shed – with, remarkably, sales never slowing down – work began on the reconstruction of the shop. Ernie began to see that the fire was offering new opportunities.

'We decided to alter the shop radically,' Ernie says. 'Geoff Davy and I had often spoken of altering the structure of the shop as its expansion over the years had created a shop with a number of rooms, not the usual layout for modern retailing.

'An architect was appointed and the flat above the shop became self-contained, with only one staircase. This opened up the interior of the shop.' They put in a brand new shop frontage such as the Barnetts had always wanted, but which had never before been a financial possibility.

Just nine months after the fire, the staff were back in their beloved shop, now renovated and refitted. They rejoiced in the phoenix-like rise from the ashes they had witnessed. The Davys were back in their refurbished flat. Everything was ready for action.

And action there was. On 1st December, 1978, a service of dedication was held at St Andrew's Bookshop. More than 100 friends gathered, spilling out onto the pavement, giving thanks to God for all He had done and giving the shop back into His hands. Fittingly, the crowd sang: 'To God be the glory, great things He hath done.' The first official customer was given place of honour – the original owner and visionary, Zettie Clark.

The great day when the newly restored bookshop was opened again on 1 December 1978.
Ernie sells the first book to the shop's founder, Zettie Clark, while Margaret looks on.

Turnover grew by more than 50 per cent. Recovery was so strong that, only a year later, Ernie and Margaret were able to spring the nicest of surprises on Lion Publishing's David and Pat Alexander. Over a meal together Ernie produced a cheque, which the Alexanders assumed was the latest instalment of the sum still outstanding on the purchase of the shop. It turned out to be the total balance owing. Within a year of apparent tragedy, the Barnetts had managed to pay off their debts and become the full owners of St Andrew's bookshop. It was a great moment.

Chapter 3
Reaching out

Expanding the work of St Andrew's Bookshop has never been purely a matter of financial turnover and profit. For Ernie and Margaret and their team, the bookshop is a ministry, a mission station, sending God's Word out into the community. Though of course, if it doesn't make a profit its ministry will soon cease.

Believing strongly in the value of Christian literature to strengthen Christians and reach the lost, the team has continually looked for ways to get it used more widely. From the earliest days book agents promoted Christian literature in scores of local churches – more on them in chapter 4.

Market stall

Soon after the Barnetts took over management of the shop, Margaret began holding book evenings at home, where people who found it difficult to get to the shop could buy literature. At Christmas 1973 a book evening overflowed into the whole week, as people kept returning to ask for books, many saying how they wished there was somewhere in the High Wycombe area where they could buy Christian books. This prompted Margaret to write to the Market Stall Manager of Wycombe District Council asking if there was a spare stall. The reply stated that she was on the waiting list.

'We prayed for an opening for nearly eight months,' she remembers. 'We as a family should have been on

holiday at the end of July but the children caught chicken-pox and so we couldn't go away. On the Monday of that week I had a phone call asking us whether we would be prepared to take a stall on Fridays from that week on and could we please let him know immediately. Well, wasn't this what we had

In all weathers Margaret and her helpers manned a Christian market stall in High Wycombe for 12 years from 1974.

Ernie talks to Jean Wilson at the 1977 meeting of the Christian Booksellers Convention, of which he is a director.

been praying for? So with fear and trepidation we said yes and went, very green and nervous, the next Friday, which was in August 1974. The other stall holders round us soon became our friends and were a great help.'

Margaret and her helpers manned the market stall each Friday for some 12 years, reaching a public who would never go into a Christian bookshop and serving people who found it difficult to get to the Great Missenden shop.

Book fairs

Christian books reach readers at coffee mornings, book parties, parents' meetings, coffee lunches and many other events where people get together. Churches and individuals have come to St Andrew's to get literature for a wide range of events over the years. Aylesbury book agents used to hold an annual Book Fair on a Saturday afternoon, widely advertised to every church within a seven-mile radius of the town. Similar fairs are held in Long Crendon, Loudwater and Haddenham.

Books at breakfast, lunch and supper

Book lovers have enjoyed many a treat when St Andrew's has brought authors to the area for a literary lunch or supper. These have included a wide diversity from Kriss Akabusi to Frank Peretti, Joyce Huggett to David Alton, Adrian Plass to Grace Shepherd. Many have been powerful times of ministry. A publisher's launch of an NIV reference Bible once made it possible to bring together 110 local church leaders from a broad spectrum for a literary breakfast.

Music evenings have been popular too, with Christian artists like Rob and Gilly Bennett performing at many concerts organised by the bookshop team. A concert with Don Francisco attracted 1,000 people.

Book evenings were held soon after the Barnetts took over the shop in order to support the book agents. They soon became very popular among regular customers, who welcomed the chance to meet authors, and helped raise the profile of St Andrew's. Many were held at Woodrow High House near Amersham, with the generous help of the Barnetts' good friend Alf Glenn.

Christian Book News

If Christians knew just what a wealth of literature was on offer, many would read more. Margaret decided to tell them. For many years the shop has compiled Christian Book News three times a year, sending it to a wide mailing list of book agents, church leaders and regular customers. It keeps them abreast of all the new Christian books and music as they are published.

This has the potential to become a major direct marketing outreach. The current list of 3,000 could be greatly expanded, with possibilities for expansion into mail order.

St Andrew's – a meeting place

Right from the start St Andrew's has played a unique role in drawing Christians together. It has attracted Christians from a wide geographical area and from an equally wide spectrum of traditions. In fact, it's so often full of folks greeting one another and having a good chat that it sometimes looks more like a social club than a business.

The various events organised by the bookshop, from literary lunches to concerts, have also played a big part in breaking down barriers.

People come here too if they want to display a notice of an open meeting, or find information on any aspect of church life. And because St Andrew's has so many links with a huge spectrum of church life, the staff are expected to know much more than just what book lives on which shelf. A caller will say they've just moved to the area and what church do you recommend. Another will ask for help with researching a talk.

People turn to the bookshop too if they want information and advice. Gos Home recalls lying in hospital in Great Missenden in 1984 having a hip replacement. He says, 'My wife and I had a broad

A large bright section of the Great Missenden shop is devoted to children's books.

Plenty of room for a wide range of stock in the extended Great Missenden bookshop.

vision of starting a Christian resources exhibition. Just a notion. I had been moved by my firm from publishing into exhibitions – and I wasn't happy about it. My wife Diane talked to Ernie about it. He said, "That's a good idea. If he wants to get a picture of what the resources are, he'd better have this book." And he gave her the *1982-83 Christian Handbook*.

'Here I was for the first time in 30 years sitting in bed with nothing to do, but my brain was working. I read the book from cover to cover. The whole thing became clear to me.'

Gos went home and wrote a brief, then summoned his chairman to dinner and sold the idea to him. It went from there. The first of many successful annual Christian Resources Exhibitions was held in 1985.

He adds, 'I doubt if the Christian Resources Exhibition would have happened without Ernie's generosity. He is a director of the Christian Booksellers Convention and could have seen the idea as a threat, but he didn't. He helped kickstart this new business which was to link the churches with their resources.'

The vision widens

The year after the re-opening of the bookshop, like every other bookseller, St Andrew's felt the chill wind of recession. The storm was weathered though, and it proved to be a matter of growth slowing down for a period rather than the severe trouble so many experienced.

Innovation and imagination in the shop's service to customers and outreach to the community were rewarded when St Andrew's won the first ever Christian Bookseller of the Year award, presented at the annual Christian Booksellers Convention in 1981. It has also won prizes for imaginative window displays.

Now Ernie and Margaret began considering the possibility of reaching out to a wider area and praying about expanding to other towns, perhaps Maidenhead.

Stephen Barnett and three of the builders support the upstairs wall during Great Missenden's expansion (see page 40).

Chapter 4
Expansion

Maidenhead

It so happened that a couple in Maidenhead were pondering about opening a bookshop. Tony and Claire Bronnimann felt the time had come to move into more direct Christian work. The door to the Anglican ministry had been pushed but did not open, and Christian friends began suggesting Tony might be the man to open a much needed Christian bookshop in Maidenhead.

Tony recalls, 'The only thing I could think to do was to ring Ernie Barnett. In July 1981 he and Margaret came over for a meal and I explained that we had the money to buy a business but no expertise. He replied that he had the expertise but no money! This was clearly one of life's godly coincidences.'

Tony discovered that his former employer's wife owned a gift shop in Maidenhead High Street, and it was now for sale. 'When we saw it,' says Ernie, 'we thought, what a super shop!' Called The Gift Box, it was well situated for High Street trade but was also a shop with a decided charm. Could this be St Andrew's first offspring?

Tony and Claire were willing to put up £10,000 towards the purchase of the business (on offer at £8,000) and the cost of

Sites of the St Andrew's Bookshops.

stocking the shop with books. After much prayer and thought, they went ahead.

They formed a company as a subsidiary of St Andrew's. Tony and Claire Bronnimann held shares and Tony also managed the shop. The staff of the two outlets began meeting regularly for prayer and fellowship.

In time the half of the shop given over to selling gifts was taken over by Christian products, and the shop was able to concentrate on the supply of Christian literature. In 1988 the ownership of the building changed hands. Tony recalls: 'The owner wished to develop the site. So it was that by God's provision, we were able to move about 30 yards to a much better shop and expand to meet the needs.

'Over the years we have been able to hold several events, most noticeably in 1991 when we held an evening with Rob and Gilly Bennett and Adrian Plass in the Town Hall. We overflowed with people, fun and laughter that evening.

'The Fisherfolk came too, in 1984, and as a result of a day conference we organised, we were able to present a cheque to Tear Fund for £715.27.

'Over the years we have been blessed by many visits: Frank Peretti, Ian White, Noel Richards, Chris Bowater, Jim Graham, Noel Proctor and many others who have given generously of their support to assist our ministry to the area.'

It was a special delight when St Andrew's Bookshop in Maidenhead was voted Christian Bookshop of the Year in 1990 in a competition run by Elm House Christian Communications.

St Andrew's (Maidenhead), with a fine central position, opened in 1981.

Reading

The Christian bookshop set up in Reading in 1967 had its origins in the charismatic movement. Founder Noel Doubleday had worked in the Fountain Trust with Michael Harper, and agreed with him in 1965 to take the Trust's bookselling work to Oxfordshire as a separate enterprise. Gateway Outreach, as it was then known, began in Witney almost exclusively as a mail order concern, selling booklets on renewal, many written by Michael Harper. Profits supported the Gateway Fellowship's ministry in Eastern Europe.

Soon, however, customers began to call in wanting to buy not only Fountain Trust booklets but Bibles and a wide range of other Christian books. In December 1967, Gateway Outreach moved to a larger location in London Street, Reading.

Bill and Anne Mercer had met Noel in Witney soon after their marriage in 1963. They became actively involved in the business in the middle 70s when Bill became a shareholder to 'mind' the business while Noel went to the USA. Anne would drive

St Andrew's (Reading), taken over in 1983, continued a long history of ministry.

from their home in Old Windsor most Wednesdays (half-day closing) to help. They took over Gateway Outreach in 1979

Anne recalls: 'We were totally ignorant of the retail trade. At this point we turned to Ernie Barnett. He so willingly gave much valued advice, support and encouragement.

'Bill's full-time job was in Twickenham and some weekday evenings, Saturdays and every bank holiday we and our three young daughters all went to Reading, complete with homework and sleeping bags, to help the original and very able manageress, Sylvia Bosher, in any way needed.

'In order to promote the shop, especially among the many schools and churches, John Brown joined the team, and later Ann Thatcher, and God really blessed the work and gave the increase.'

In 1983 when the Mercers moved to the Isle of Wight turnover was exceeding all

The interior of St Andrew's, Reading.

expectations. As it was impossible to oversee from such a distance, they offered the business to Ernie, and it joined the group of shops as St Andrew's (Reading). The name Gateway Outreach then returned to the mission which in the meantime had been incorporated into Open Doors with Brother Andrew.

The shop now needed a new manager. Fred Hammond recalls: 'December 1983 saw my wife Sheila and daughter Jane both working as staff at the bookshop. Little did I know that this shop in London Street, Reading, was to be very much a part of God's plan for my continuing working life.

'I was serving as a Principal Officer at Reading Prison with almost 25 years service. Now at 55 I was eligible to consider early retirement but I had decided to defer retirement for at least two years.

'Late one afternoon during January 1984 I called at the Christian Bookshop to collect Sheila and Jane. While waiting I began to browse round the shelves. A man came over to me and said politely, "Can I help you?"

'When I told him I was only waiting for Sheila and Jane, he said: "You must be Fred, Sheila's husband. How would you like to come and work for me?"

'I did not know at the time of the plans of the company to engage a full-time manager. I realised that this must be Ernie Barnett, the managing director of St Andrew's Bookshops and replied: "I don't know about that."

'I did not consider this meeting with Ernie to be a divine appointment, but looking back on the events that followed I believe it was.

'As we left Ernie came to the door with us and asked me to consider the prospect of working at St Andrew's Bookshop. I said I would pray about it.'

'As we were going home in the car my wife said: "Surely you are not going to think about working at the shop? It certainly would not be beneficial to us."

'I said: "Don't worry, it probably won't happen", but I did say I would pray about it.

'I knew I could ill afford to leave a well-paid job for the much lower pay as bookshop manager, and I had a mortgage to consider.'

Soon after Fred found himself at a prison officers'

training course in Yorkshire. During the first week there God reminded him of his promise to pray about the job possibility at St Andrew's.

His Bible reading in Genesis highlighted how God changed Joseph's difficulties into exceptional opportunities. 'Three words in Genesis 46.3 spoke forcibly to me, "I am God". What about that bookshop position?

'I talked to my wife at the weekend, and soon with virtually no experience of the retail trade I was interviewed and selected to fulfil a completely new role. So I resigned from the Prison Service and took up my new appointment in March 1984.

'Initially it was a time of learning but in due course I began to become accustomed to the responsibilities which were now mine and I relished the challenges this presented.

'I was encouraged by Selwyn Hughes' words about "turning setbacks into stepping stones". Much help and ready advice came from Ernie.'

By 1992-93 the turnover had risen from £148,000 to £227,000. The shop set out to establish good relationships with local churches, promoting books through book agencies, and supporting church events. The shop front was updated,

A mother with two young customers at St Andrew's.

and staff were encouraged to read widely to equip them in recommending books to meet customers' needs.

'Disappointments were far outweighed by the many blessings. At least one person came to know the Lord in the shop.

'One day we received a letter containing a postal order. It read simply: "I came to your shop some time ago and took a book from your shelves and did not pay for it. I read the book and as a result God changed my life and I became a Christian. I enclose the cost of the book."

'Until I retired at the end of 1993 I was privileged to work with dedicated staff who sought to walk daily with the

Lord and set a high standard of commitment. Each morning before opening the shop a time of prayer took place.

'Husbands and wives working together was something Ernie and Margaret set out to do from the day the Great Missenden shop opened, followed by Tony and Claire Bronnimann at Maidenhead and then Sheila and myself at Reading. It worked exceptionally well and still does.

'I also served as a director until May 1996. It has been a privilege to be involved in the Christian book ministry and to know at first hand the important part books play in the Christian life.'

Wolverton

St Andrew's Bookshop in Wolverton has its roots in the twin shops set up by Lion Publishing as distribution centres for their own titles. One was St Andrew's in Great Missenden, where Ernie started his bookshop life as manager. The other was in Stony Stratford.

Its manager David Rudiger later took the shop, Aslan Books, and moved it to Bletchley in 1983, where it included a coffee shop, but the position was far from ideal and it struggled to be viable. David approached Ernie and in 1987 the shop became a branch of St Andrew's. When the lease came up for renewal in 1990 the shop moved to Wolverton, just north of Milton Keynes, resulting in a doubling of turnover.

The ideal site would be in the Milton Keynes' main shopping complex, but the rents are prohibitive. Yet the present shop is a smart outlet close to a shopping centre and bus station. Christians search it out, and its staff member Linda Winstanley commented: 'Our shop offers the best selection of greeting cards in the locality and that draws in a lot of passing trade. It's surprising too how many non-Christians come in to buy prayer cards and other small cards with mottoes and poems.'

The Wolverton shop, a St Andrew's outlet since 1987, serves the Milton Keynes area.

Oxford

A secret of success in any Christian ministry must be to have the right staff, and Ernie believes God has always sent along the right personnel at the right time.

Paul Crockett, for example, was wondering if God could use his skills more directly, two years after becoming a Christian. Paul had 15 years experience in the book trade working for W. H. Smith. He 'happened' to mention this to Ernie just at the point when St Andrew's was considering buying the two bookshops at St Clement's and St Ebbe's in Oxford. (St Clement's is on the outskirts of the city, and St Ebbe's in the town centre near a major shopping precinct.) Before long, in 1991, Paul found himself manager of the two Oxford shops and the Witney shop.

He says: 'It was good to be able to put my experience of systems and management in the book trade to better use in a Christian environment.

'I had a lot to learn, of course, about the range and depth of Christian books.'

Paul discovered that Christian books cover a range of quality: 'Some areas are very good – biographies, books on the Christian life. Others are amateurish in the writing but written from the heart, and you can feel the Holy Spirit come through even if they may not stand up as works of literature.'

One difference between secular and Christian book buying, he finds, is that in the secular market, an author becomes popular and people buy all their books. In the Christian book trade it's the subject matter that's more important.

St Andrew's Bookshop at St Clement's, Oxford, opened in 1991, continues a long tradition of literature ministry.

A ministry of Christian literature has taken place at the St Clement's shop since 1948, when the Gospel Book Depot was set up with Christopher Quarterman as its first chairman and co-founder. Warren Eccles ran the business from 1969 to 1991.

Recession

The early 90s saw recession biting hard. Christian bookshops around the country joined the toll of businesses which were forced to close. St Andrew's Bookshops began losing money instead of making a profit, but were able to keep going through the strength of now being a large operation. But it's been a painful time – especially when in 1995 for the first time two members of staff had to be made redundant.

It's been a question of 'tightening belts', diligent application of efficiency measures, and gratitude that the group is big enough to bring the advantage of centralised buying. They were grateful to find themselves back in profit for the year 1995-96.

St Ebbe's is centrally placed in Oxford for students and shoppers.

Witney

In 1992 both the Congregational and Methodist churches in Witney were making major alterations to their buildings, and St Andrew's was approached about perhaps setting up a branch in one of these sites. After discussion and prayer this proved impractical, but the Congregational church asked how they could encourage St Andrew's to find another outlet in the town. A joint venture was worked out, which proved a wonderful example of a church and business working together to provide a town with an outlet for Christian literature.

Today the shop in the old part of the church is an ideal site in the busy High Street with ample free parking nearby. It opened in October 1994 and results so far have been most encouraging with good support from the local community. Although not big enough to meet all the needs of the local community, the shop is willing to order what is not in stock to meet the needs of customers.

Because of the success of this venture, similar opportunities are being explored in other towns. By mid-1996 St Andrew's was planning to open a small outlet within Holm Grange Craft Village at Wokingham, which is likely to prove an outreach centre for spreading Christian literature among the general public.

The Christian bookshop in Witney joined the St Andrew's family in 1994.

The High Street, Witney, Oxfordshire.

New opportunities

A major bonus in recent years has been the opportunity for St Andrew's to provide bookstalls at a number of major conferences and fairs. At 1996's New Wine and Soul Survivor conference, for example, the bookstall took £100,000 in three weeks – equal to a month's trade at all seven shops.

Similar opportunities have been welcomed to provide books at Soul Survivor, Pioneer churches' conference, the Christian Resources Exhibition at Birmingham and Esher, the Mainstream Baptist conference at Swanwick, Headway summer camp, and Salt and Light. Ernie says: 'They are a valuable source of income, and are part of a wider ministry that St Andrew's is increasingly involved in.'

The growth of Alpha courses in British churches has also generated tremendous sales among people who weren't reading Christian books before.

A new opportunity to promote the bookshops and Christian music came when Radio ElevenSeventy was launched in High Wycombe, a Christian backed radio station. St Andrew's sponsored a Monday evening slot called Soul and Spirit devoted to Christian music from 1994 to 1995.

The Net Book Agreement, which brought a shiver to secular bookshops, is not such a threat to Christian bookshops, Ernie believes: 'Shops tend to be so far apart, and people aren't likely to travel 20 miles to save £2.' On the other hand, it does give greater freedom with pricing, for example making it possible to launch new titles with introductory offers.

St Andrew's along with others took part in the Christian Book Festival, which held its first programme in May-June 1996. This nationwide initiative by publishers and bookshops aims to raise the profile of Christian books and reading. It marks a new determination to challenge Christians to use the wealth of resources available both for their personal growth and for greater effectiveness in mission.

Under the slogan Read for your Life! St Andrew's Bookshops got together with the Bible Reading Fellowship, Lion Publishing and Oxford University Press to celebrate Christian books. The highlight was an address by Lord Coggan at a service in Oxford on 29 May.

The shop next door

The expansion to other towns and development of bookstalls at big Christian events were now putting pressure on St Andrew's warehouse capacity. The warehouse currently in use was about to become unavailable. Just at the right time the lease on the shop next door to St Andrew's on Great Missenden High Street came up for sale, a greengrocer's. As well as the front shop, it had a number of outbuildings at the back which could be developed into offices and stores.

After much prayer and some hesitation, as well as discussions with professional friends, in 1993 it was decided to appeal to the shop's supporters for loans. About 60 loyal friends of St Andrew's gave gifts and loans, with or without interest.

Ernie recalls: 'We appealed for £250,000, on reflection possibly the wrong amount. But God in his goodness prompted his people to provide approximately £60,000. This was just enough for the alteration work to be carried out.'

Tony Bronnimann oversaw the rebuilding, which created some fear and trembling at some points, such as when the ancient walls had to be supported while a new floor was put in.

The re-opening day was a great occasion, with Terry Waite carrying out the ceremony and the then Bishop of Buckingham Simon Burrows leading the prayer of dedication.

Terry was in the middle of a high-profile tour of Britain promoting his book *Taken on Trust* and talking about his experiences in captivity in the Lebanon. After cutting the ribbon he led the crowd of wellwishers to Great Missenden Church where he spoke. More than 200 of his books were sold that day.

St Andrew's provides bookstalls at a number of major conferences.

Staff

The Barnetts were surprised, and pleased, when their middle son Steve announced he would like to work in the shop. He had just completed a BA in economics and geography. Ten years later he has proved his worth, and is responsible for all the buying for the group as well as showing vision and enthusiasm for future development. He also organises much of the conference work.

The directors now are Ernie and Margaret, their son Steve as sales and marketing director, Tony Bronnimann, retail director, and Norman Nibloe, chairman of the Christian Booksellers Convention. The company secretary is Nick Jones, who is managing director of Candle Books.

Keith Lewis worked part-time at the shop as financial director after retiring as assistant chief accountant for Midland Bank, until he moved to Derby in 1991, and Fred Hammond, formerly Reading

Terry Waite opened the extended bookshop in Great Missenden in 1993.

shop manager, retired as a director in 1996.

St Andrew's is now a widespread group of sister shops, benefiting from centralised administration. Staff get together occasionally for an away-day, and once every two years all the staff have a Christmas get-together.

While the rest of the business community responded to the pressures of the recession in the early 90s with 'downsizing' and minimising overheads, St Andrew's too was forced to make painful decisions as profits fell. The comfortable sense of it being a family business run with a staff of friends had to give way to greater professionalism. Over the past five years the need for strong management structures has led to the appointment of a marketing and sales director, the part-time employment of a management consultant, the introduction of computers, and the expansion of the Great Missenden shop to accommodate a proper accounts office and meeting room.

Staff, of course, are crucial to the success of any bookshop. Asked what are the characteristics of a good member of staff, Ernie says: 'A knowledge of theology is very useful and a pleasant personality is vital. They must be able to keep calm under pressure and be quick to learn. Integrity is important and a genuine desire to satisfy the customer always adds that bit extra. A good memory is also helpful.'

It sounds like a tall order, especially in view of the low rate of pay that retailers are able to offer. But St Andrew's has been blessed with fine people over the years who have served the shops and their customers loyally.

At the Christian Booksellers Convention 1996: (front) Ernie and a German friend;
(middle) Margaret, Katie Debano, Sheila Hammond, Mary Perry, Claire Curtis;
(back) Ruth Palmer, Steve Barnett, Rosemary Vickery, Elizabeth Gardiner, Melvyn Gardiner, Paul Cromwell.

St Andrew's Church, Chorleywood.

Right: Bishop David Pytches, formerly Vicar of St Andrew's, Chorleywood.

Chapter 5
Paper Pastors and Book Agents

Christian books can be 'paper missionaries', spreading the Good News. They are also 'paper pastors', bringing teaching, encouragement and support to Christians.

Many people who feel that public speaking is not their gift welcome the chance to be involved in a literature ministry. Others who are involved in more direct evangelism find that the Christian book is an extension of their ministry – it can go home with an enquirer or new Christian, and continue to teach about Christ in days to come.

In some 250 churches and Christian groups served by St Andrew's Bookshops, someone is supplying this need, seeing it as their form of service to make Christian books available in the neighbourhood. In most cases the bookstall is on display in church after services, and perhaps at events like Sunday school parents' meetings or youth rallies.

Book agencies vary from a small box of books, to a large bookshop in its own right.

They start with a small stock of literature collected from St Andrew's on a sale-or-exchange basis. This facility is not extended by all Christian bookshops as it involves a tremendous amount of work for staff, but St Andrew's has operated this way for nearly 40 years, much to the benefit of book agents. They are given 10 per cent discount on books sold.

Most take up the role because they themselves find books valuable in their Christian lives. And they need to be familiar with what's on offer in order to meet the many queries that come their way:

'My neighbour's husband has just left her – what book do you think might be helpful?'

'The youngster next door is going to university, and I'd like to give him something.'

'My non-Christian friend is in hospital. I want a biography with a message, but so gripping that she won't be able to put it down.'

Chorleywood

Books are high profile at St Andrew's Church at Chorleywood. They are displayed on shelving in the vestibule, and can be used any time the church is open – which is every day and many evenings. It's not manned, and people put the money into a wall safe. But the office staff can see through to the book shelves and notice if anything is amiss. Last year it sold £45,000 worth of books, cards and tapes.

The secret of a book-buying congregation, says Rosemary Vickery, who took over the bookstall 15 years ago, lies with church leaders: 'Our leaders read. And they continually recommend books from the pulpit and refer to books in their sermons.' It also helps that both Bishop David Pytches and his wife Mary are successful authors in their own right.

Stocking a good range of Christian greetings cards also brings in a lot of buyers during the week from other churches. The bookstall holds £10,000 worth of stock owned by the church. The church treasurer handles all the bills, and profits go straight to church funds.

Large numbers of books are sold six times a year when up to 300 leaders from around the country meet at St Andrew's Church for leaders' conferences: 'We can take £1,000 a day. Many leaders are great book buyers but don't have book agencies at their own churches.'

Aylesbury

There is no book display at the Church of the Good Shepherd in Aylesbury, but Kath Webb has run a book agency there for 18 years with a turnover of £2,000 a year. It works through 'plugging' books occasionally during the service, and spreading news of any interesting books or seasonal specials. Kath also supplies Bible reading notes and Sunday school materials.

She also supplies books to the Aylesbury Religious Resources Centre, where member individuals, churches and schools can borrow books, videos, charts, sets of books and other materials.

Some of the profits from the book agency are used to give a discount to people who find it difficult to afford their Bible reading notes, and to those training for the ministry.

Beaconsfield

A neat little bookshop within the coffee shop set up by Beaconsfield churches is a convenient place for passersby to buy books and cards. Pat Ward says, 'It's the only place in Beaconsfield to buy Christian literature and gifts, so it's especially busy at Christmas. People welcome the chance to buy Bible reading notes here, which is an important ministry. And they often come in looking for little books to give to friends or relatives to meet a particular need such as bereavement.'

Chalfont St Peter

Gold Hill Baptist Church runs The Myrtle Tree, a coffee shop with Christian bookshop in the nearby village of Chalfont St Peter, as well as a bookshop joined to the church.

The one at the church is open six half-days a week and for half an hour before and after the Sunday service. It operates with 13 volunteers.

The Sunday Trading Bill caused some heart-searching. Bookshop organiser Rita Harris, a retired teacher, says, 'We used to be open on Sundays, but when the Sunday Trading Bill was going through, the church was vocal on the issue and we stopped opening on Sundays. Now we just open for a short while before and after Sunday services. We find that people who live nearby come to the shop in the week, while those who come some distance to church welcome the chance to buy books while they are here.'

The bookshop sees its ministry as not only to serve church members' needs, but to get Christian literature into schools and libraries using the shop's profits of some £4,000 a year. The shop's gift tokens are donated to 13 local schools and two libraries, so they can choose their own books. And all the church's missionaries receive a gift token when they arrive home on furlough so they can replenish their own bookshelves.

Rita says, 'The bookshop has a wider ministry than just selling books, stationery and tapes. Often people call in to talk, and it's amazing how often just the right people are on duty to meet their needs.'

Gold Hill Baptist Church also runs The Myrtle Tree in the nearby village of Chalfont St Peter. The coffee shop is widely used, and people have to come through the shop to reach it. The small display includes greetings cards and gifts as well as Bibles and Christian books. Pam Kerr says: 'The shop is very much part of our church outreach. We have quite a regular clientele, and the coffee shop and bookshop staff get together to pray for customers whom we get to know. A number

Staff from St Andrew's Bookshops at the Christian Booksellers Convention in 1987:
(from left) Ernie Barnett, Margaret Preston, Fred Hammond, Sheila Hammond, Vera Gibbons, Margaret Barnett,
Claire Bronnimann, Christine Wallhouse, Steve Barnett, David Rudiger, Tony Bronnimann.

have come to the Lord through The Myrtle Tree, and many say it's the friendly atmosphere that attracts them to come in. We were very cheered recently when an AA tearoom guide said very nice things about us!'

Ernie adds: 'The book agents have done a wonderful job over the years in making Christian literature accessible to people in the churches. We particularly value our continuing partnership with the bookshops at St Andrew's Church at Chorleywood, Gold Hill Baptist and the Myrtle Tree, and Beaconsfield Coffee Shop, as well as the King's Church Bookshop in High Wycombe until it closed in 1994. So many of these book agents have become our friends.'

Chapter 6
What's the Point of Books?

The writing of books was inaugurated by God himself after a battle when the Amalekites tried to destroy Israel: 'And the Lord said to Moses, write this for a memorial in a book' (Exodus 17.14).

Billy Strachan of Capernwray Bible School once commented: 'God is aware that not only is man fallen and in sin, but he now lives with a fallen memory, unable to retain or recall what he ought to be able to. Thus books were to be an essential part of life to educate his people in order that they might not be destroyed by their enemies.'

Books were also to keep us from error, as in the life of David (1 Chronicles 15.13-15). Books were responsible for a massive revival (2 Chronicles 34). The existence of the Jews today is due to books (Esther 6.1).

Billy Strachan added: 'It might well be that for the Christian who seeks more protection, correction, revival and security, the answer lies not in something new from God, but in Paul's admonition to Timothy, "Study to show thyself approved." More reading, less preaching.'

Norman Burrows, retired Methodist minister and prison visitor, and his wife Betty.

Books in prison

Christian literature has been a crucially important tool for Norman Burrows. Now retired after a lifetime as Methodist minister and prison visitor, Norman says, 'Books have been invaluable in my ministry. I have always bought a lot and loaned them out. New converts, people struggling over issues, anyone in trouble – as well as trying to help them myself, I ask God to lead me to the right book to lend them. I've seen books change people's lives.'

Books were particularly important when Norman visited prisons, where there is no lack of time for reading. He would always have half a dozen books stuffed into his pocket. 'Some inmates were great

Staff from St Andrew's Bookshops at the Christian Booksellers Convention in 1989: (from left, front) Ernie, Margaret, Sheila Hammond; (back) Ann Shepherd, Claire Bronnimann, Steve Barnett, Alf Glenn, David Rudiger, Janet White, Linda Winstanley, Fred Hammond, Sue Gibbs, Nika Vassiliou.

readers and would get through a book a week. Others had never read at all. They really welcomed the chance to borrow a book. And it also was invaluable the next time I visited, as we could chat about the book they'd read.

'The most popular books were what I call the Christian thrillers – books like *Prison to Praise, God's Prison Gang, The Cross and the Switchblade*.'

Another prison visitor, who works at a young offenders' institution near Aylesbury, also finds Christian books very welcome. She maintains a stock of books in the chapel that inmates can borrow. One lad was converted in his cell after reading the book *Run Baby Run*, and many young Christians are helped in their walk with God through the ministry of Christian literature.

The answer

Margaret Strutt turned to a booklet when she felt a desire to turn to God, but didn't know how to set about it. Both her sons came home from university having found God, and set about evangelising their parents Margaret and Peter. Margaret recalls, 'At our eldest son's confirmation, the Holy Spirit worked in a remarkable way and I knew that I had to commit my life to Christ. But how?

'More in hope than expectation I took myself off to St Andrew's Bookshop and there found the answer in a little booklet, *Journey Into Life*. That little book was the key which made it possible for the whole family to become Christians and changed our lives for ever.'

From jumble to joy

Roy and Maureen Hurd of Beaconsfield found salvation in their early fifties through a book picked up at a jumble sale. The book Maureen brought home was *Power for Living* by Jamie Buckingham. She said: 'It convicted me, and explained about God's forgiveness, and I was converted through reading it.

'Then I bought *How to be Born Again* by Billy

Graham at the book shop in Beaconsfield coffee shop and handed it to my husband. He read it and was converted too. We were nominal Christians before, but had shut God out of our lives.

'My whole life was totally changed. I used to be an avid reader of novels, now I want to read Christian books. I enjoy ones like *Hind's Feet on High Places* – any that draw you to the Lord.'

You are what you read

Lay preacher Ray Scorey says, 'Our book shelves depict a lot of our character and experience. We tend to keep books that have meant a lot to us in our Christian walk. They are like an Ebenezer, reminding us of where God taught us something special. Books that have been important to me include *Prison to Praise* and Mary Batchelor's *Seasons of Life*. It's always good to turn back to a book that was a help to us in bringing us through some situation.'

Moving on

One wintry day in 1983 Tony Felman visited the bookshop in Great Missenden with his wife. Just before reaching the door he slipped over and crashed to the pavement. He ended up in hospital with a cracked pelvis and damage to his hip.

'I had to stay in bed at home for two weeks then take it easy. It's very rare that I've had to stay in bed, but this time there was no choice.

'I had given my life to Jesus three years earlier but hadn't moved on much in that time. The Lord was giving me a thirst for the Word of God but I was too busy to find time. This fall humbled me and forced me to stay in bed. I spent the time reading the Book of Revelation together with Hal Lindsay's *There's a New World Coming*. It really blessed me and the Spirit moved me on in an incredible way. It awakened a great interest in end-time teaching and gave me the desire to read the Word more. Since then I've studied it regularly.'

Old truth, new angle

Ian Stackhouse, pastor of The King's Church Amersham, believes books help Christians to engage the mind and the heart in a more reflective way. They bring new perspectives.

While acknowledging that television has discouraged reading, he believes that pastors and church leaders can make a difference by recommending books.

Christian books have certainly been important in his own life and ministry. They bring new angles on old truths, and are important ways of enabling leaders to feed themselves spiritually. Tozer was a favourite in his early days as a Christian, and Ian adds: 'Many times I have been blessed by a book or article. I find St Andrew's gives excellent service and a very warm atmosphere. The staff are tremendous servants to the church.'

Pastor Ian Stackhouse with one of his sons.

Over the next few years Tony's job in overseas marketing gave him ample time to read during flights to other countries.

Books and ministry

Bishop David Pytches, formerly Vicar of St Andrew's, Chorleywood, highlights the importance of Christian books in his own life and his ministry. He says, 'My own call to the mission field (I spent 17 years in Latin America) was inspired through reading missionary books, as was my openness to the power of the Holy Spirit when we first encountered it ourselves in St Andrew's.

'Christian books are still important to me as they are so helpful for my own spiritual journey, my preaching and my writing.

'At St Andrew's Church we promote the reading of Christian books because it's one of the best ways to learn about both the basics of the Christian faith and also some more profound doctrines, and its practical outworking through testimony. We think it helps to see what other churches and denominations are doing, both here and in other parts of the world, and this is communicated through books.

'It is so useful to know just the right book to give to the right people at the right time. If one doesn't read, one doesn't know what book to give.

'We owe a great deal to St Andrew's Bookshop through their constant supply to our church and conferences.'

Not a job but a ministry

Evangelist J. John highlighted the value of books when he addressed the Christian Booksellers' Convention in March 1996. He emphasised that the work of the Christian book trade was a crucially important ministry.

His talk was based on II Timothy 4:13 where Paul writes: 'When you come bring my coat, the books too.'

J. John quoted Spurgeon's comment: 'He is inspired, yet he wants books. He has been preaching at least 30 years, he has seen the Lord, yet he wants books. He has a wider experience than most people, yet he wants books. He has been caught up to heaven and heard things which it is unlawful to utter, yet he wants books. He has written the major part of the New Testament, yet he wants books.' Even in Paul's old age, in the final phase of his ministry, he wanted to keep reading.

Oswald Sanders wrote: 'The person who desires to grow spiritually and intellectually will be constantly at their books.'

John Wesley read thousands of books on horseback as he travelled in his ministry.

J. John continued: 'Selling books is a ministry, and I want to commend you all in the book world, and to encourage you to see your work not as a job, but as a great joy, because books are important and we should do all we can to encourage reading.

'We read them for inspiration and motivation. William Law wrote: "Reading on wise and virtuous subjects is, next to the Bible and prayer, the best improvement of our hearts. It enlightens us, it calms us, it collects our thoughts, and prompts us to better efforts. We say, a man is known by the friends he keeps. But a man is known even better by his books."

Evangelist J. John.

'I feel personally that few things get me out of sluggishness better than reading a good book. So I read for inspiration. We should never underestimate the power of a book.

'I also read to sharpen my skills. Reading is to the mind what exercise is to the body.

'We also read to learn from others. Yes, of course we all learn from the school of hard knocks, of trial and error. It's wise to learn from experience, wiser to learn from others.

'Socrates said: "Employ your time in improving yourselves by other people's documents. So shall you come easily by what others have laboured hard for." Doesn't that make sense?

'By reading books we interact with people we've never met, we get to see how the great minds think, we sit in the company of great people by reading biographies. I've been influenced by people who died even before I was born. Many from the past have become my mentors as I have read their books.

'Books are a gift from God. I think TV is the greatest enemy to reading today.

'If we set aside 30 minutes a day we will read 45 books a year, so in 25 years we will have read 1,000 books. That is equivalent to going to college full-time five times.

'We need to balance our reading. Carnegie wrote: "A man's reading programme should be as carefully planned as his daily diet, for that is food without which he cannot grow mentally." Our biggest mistake often is to concentrate on our favourite field or our favourite topic, like reading our favourite passages in the Bible. It's good to read widely.

'We shouldn't just read the book. We should respond to it. What am I supposed to do with this knowledge?

'We need to know what to read. Be discriminating. James Brye wrote: "Life is too short to spend it reading inferior books."

'I read one hour a day, one evening a week, one day a month, one week a year. Do you know why? Because I asked John Stott 16 years ago how often he read, and that's what he said. That gets me through four books a week. I love them.

'We must not forget the Bible. The Bible is a lantern to our feet. It is a light to our path. (And the Bible sheds a lot of light on a lot of commentaries!)

'You have been entrusted with the ministry of making books available and accessible. Why? All because of Jesus, for Jesus, to Jesus.'

Words that change lives

Today as throughout Christian history, the Word of God and books based on the Word are changing lives.

Samuel Zwemer claimed, 'No agency can penetrate so deeply, witness so daringly, abide so persistently and influence so daringly as the printed page.

Or as Robert Murray McCheyne put it, 'The smallest tract may be the stone in David's sling. In the hands of Christ it may bring down a giant soul.'

The printed page, it's been said, is a visitor who gets inside the home and stays there; it always catches a man in the right mood, for it speaks to him only when he is reading it.

There are many stories to be told of how books have been paper missionaries. The rest of this chapter is taken, with permission, from a Christian Literature Crusade leaflet, *Why Read Christian Books?*

• A lawyer involved in the Watergate scandal became friendly with a man called Tom Phillips. Tom read to him a passage from *Mere Christianity* by C. S. Lewis. 'As he read I could feel a flush coming into my face and a curious burning sensation . . . Lewis's words seemed to pound straight at me.'

He took the book on vacation with him and read it through. He was challenged by it and by the end of that week he had made a commitment to Christ which sustained him through what was to come. The lawyer was Chuck Colson. His story can be found in *Born Again*.

• Selwyn Hughes wrote: 'Although I am constantly involved in preaching and teaching I have been encouraged more through the response to the printed word than by any other means. No one anywhere on this planet would have a higher regard for the power of Christian literature than I. With me it is one of the highest priorities – for prayer and action.'

• John Collins, a clergyman in Oxford, used the booklet *Becoming a Christian* by John Stott to explain the message of Christ to a young man.

He found the book 'compelling with its simplicity and clear in its logical reasoning'. It was part of the process which led him to accept Christ as his personal Saviour. The young man? David Watson.

• In prison in Thailand for the possession of heroin, Rita Nightingale was on the edge of despair. Alone in her cell, looking for a handkerchief she found a booklet left by a visitor. The book was called *The Reason Why*, by Robert Laidlaw. In her own words: 'I began to read. As I read, it seemed as if every word in the booklet had been written with me in mind . . .' Her book *Freed for Life* tells how she committed her life to Christ.

• Philip Mohabir recounts in his book *Building Bridges*: '"Follow ME and I will make you fishers of men" Mark 1:17. Like a sharp arrow well aimed, these words leapt out from the pages of my text-book and pierced my heart.

'As I read, I became aware of a strange Presence and the whole atmosphere changed. The classroom became a holy place. It was as though Jesus stood there gazing down at me. Something different was happening to me. His eyes, gentle, loving eyes which went right through me, left me feeling exposed and naked. It was as though time stopped . . . I could hear a soft yet authoritative voice deep inside me saying, "Follow me . . ." It was gentle yet irresistible.'

• Brian Greenaway, a member of a Hell's Angel chapter, was in prison. Each week one of the prison visitors brought in a copy of the *Methodist Recorder*. Brian read it because it was free.

He was intrigued by a regular advertisement for a new Bible – *The Living Bible*. Eventually he asked the visitor for a copy, and was given one along with another book, *Run Baby Run*.

He started the book first: 'It was the true story of a New York gang leader. But it was as though I was reading my story. The places were different but the violence, sex and drugs and crime were the same.' He kept on reading and committed his life there in his cell. His story is told in the book *Hell's Angel*.

• 'That's it! That's it! I'm a son of God! It was like a great flash of light,' wrote Colin Urquhart in *When the Spirit Comes*. 'Something I had been searching for had suddenly been discovered. I'm a son of God! That truth transformed my life and ministry.

'I was reading a book, *The Normal Christian Life*, written by a Chinese layman with the unlikely name of Watchman Nee. This made me realise that nearly everything I had known and experienced about the Christian life was "sub-normal".'

• A. W. Tozer wrote, 'The function of a good book is to stand like a signpost directing the reader toward the Truth and the Life . . . The work of a good book is to incite the reader to moral action, to turn his eyes toward God and urge him forward.'

Chapter 7
I'd like to run a Christian bookshop . . .

It's a vision with plenty of appeal for many people: a flourishing little Christian bookshop in a small town, at the centre of church life, serving local Christians and ministering to their needs, while providing a focus for outreach and evangelism and providing God's people with the tools to do the job.

There is no shortage of Christians who would like to give their lives to such a venture, and many have made their way to Ernie Barnett's door over the years. After all, St Andrew's is just such a story, a work for God which had small beginnings and grew to a widespread ministry, and there are other shops too which have succeeded under God's hand in a similar way.

Frequently as Ernie has sat down and discussed people's plans with them, many have said they had no capital and saw their venture as a work of faith. He has had to point out that to set up a shop in a professional way today, you would need £50,000 to £100,000 of capital to fit and stock the shop with some working capital.

It's sometimes necessary to paint a picture of harsh realism. Ernie points out: 'The changes in the Christian book trade have been quite remarkable since St Andrew's began. During those 40 years many folk have dreamed of running a shop, believing that every town should have its own, without realising the difficulties involved in sustaining such a work and keeping it financially viable.'

Christian bookshops have all the problems of any other retailer – assessing customer demands, stock levels, cashflow, overheads including rent, rates and wages. Just like any other shop they must be in profit if they are to keep afloat.

And while some Christians may view the setting up of a Christian bookshop as a ministry, once open most of the public view it like any other retailer. With the demise of the Net Book Agreement, competition on price and service can only increase.

One change which has affected Christian bookshop sales is the Sunday school prize market. It was far more active 40 years ago, when most churches ran their own schools and presented each child with a book each year. Many readers will have memories of the hardback editions of children's books published by Victory Press and Pickering & Inglis at 2/6, 3/- and 3/6, with a print-run lasting perhaps five years.

Today, publishing is based on an initial print run lasting no more than 18 months and then remaindered.

In the 40 years of St Andrew's work the volume of titles being produced annually has increased dramatically. Over-production and importation of titles has led to volumes of books far in excess of what the trade can cope with.

The quantity of titles being produced has been at the expense of quality, a result of publishers' hope that new titles will keep turnover up. Some wonder whether lack of quality is the reason for the static state of the market, with customers disappointed with the choice available.

Of course some titles have been constant bestsellers

over recent decades, among them *The Lion Handbook to the Bible*, Adrian Plass titles, *The Hiding Place*, *The Cross and the Switchblade*. Today there seem to be fewer bestsellers being produced that end up in the realm of classics.

On the other hand, the attractiveness of books has increased enormously, particularly with the development of co-edition publishing with overseas publishers in several languages. This makes it possible for print-runs to be in the region of perhaps 50,000 copies, at lower cost. It also enables countries with small Christian communities to have good quality books in their own language.

It is impossible to stock even a fraction of the titles available. Yet it often seems when a customer wants a book today, they order tomorrow and come in yesterday to collect it.

Like other retailing, it is a low-pay business, but requires people with a retentive mind, patience and some theological knowledge.

Another aspect of Christian bookselling which is a blessing in terms of outreach but a headache administratively is book agents. Their work is vital in getting books to readers, but the 10 per cent agent's discount does drain some of the profitability of the shop. St Andrew's has always offered its agents a sale-and-exchange facility.

Surveys show that there is a decline in Christian reading, even regular reading of the Bible. Today Christian retail trade sales are split 70 per cent books, 10 per cent cards, and 20 per cent cassettes, CDs and miscellaneous items.

All too many Christian bookshops have fallen prey to the pressures of the market place. Some have closed, others manage to keep going with turnovers of less than £50,000 only through the dedicated work of their staff.

Today there are 579 Christian bookshops in the UK, with an average turnover of £75,000 for smaller shops (less than 93 sq m) and £168,000 among the larger ones. Most are independent shops, with a handful of chains operating on a regional scale, like St Andrew's, and larger chains operating on a national scale, such as CLC, SPCK and Wesley Owen (the largest, owned by STL, with more than 35 branches).

In the case of St Andrew's, as it has developed into a chain of shops the more profitable outlets have made it possible to keep open the less profitable ones in a time of acute financial pressure.

Ernie says: 'As we publish our story, trade continues to be difficult but the need to make significant books available to speak to this world of great need is still as pressing as ever.'

Ernie Barnett (left) at St Ebbe's shop, Oxford.

Chapter 8
Is the Book Finished?

Electronic communication, the World-Wide Web, interactive media – all these buzzwords are said to spell the death of the printed page. So are we witnessing the last gasps of the Age of the Book?

Predictions vary. Some say the current forebodings on the decay of literature are merely end-of-century doom-mongering. The same was said, they point out, in the final years of the 19th Century.

Others are pessimistic about the fate of reading in an electronic age. They predict the imminent disappearance of the reader.

But the death of reading, if it comes at all, is taking its time. After all, film and TV were said to augur the end of books. It didn't happen. Indeed, videos and TV versions of books tend to promote book reading rather than replace it.

Audiotapes, or talking books, have certainly had an impact on publishing generally. But here again, publishers are tending to produce the two together rather than replace the book with the tape.

And do you remember the interactive book, which a decade ago was predicted to be sounding the death knell of the printed page? With on-screen books you could direct the plot and choose your own ending. Apart from the dungeons-and-dragons type of story game, however, these have scarcely taken off.

More tempting to the average reader might be the story on-screen where you can pull in a colour photo of the scene described, or a video clip adding authenticity to a travel or history book. This is certainly part of the appeal of the current race to put newspapers onto the Internet.

CD-ROM offers access to information that was unthinkable a generation ago. A disk far smaller than a paperback book can hold the whole *Encyclopaedia Britannica* and more, plus access to thousands of still pictures, video clips and sound to illustrate the text.

And the Internet opens a door into libraries world-wide.

Yet still there is nothing like the cosy pleasure of a book in your hand.

As electronic media get more sophisticated, there have certainly been effects on the style of books. This century has seen the printed word becoming crisper, briefer, less elite, more user-friendly. But what will the future hold?

US professor of English Elaine Showalter wrote in *The Guardian*, 'I can imagine a paperback-size computer on which you could call up any book. When it arrives on your screen, you could also have the option of an on-line discussion group, composed of other readers – a reading club in cyberspace.

'Book stores are evolving away from being libraries with price tags towards becoming cultural centres, with cafes, author appearances, debates, computer specialists, community groups and activities for children. My local bookstores in Princeton, New Jersey, for instance, now provide everything from Sunday brunch and the London newspapers to poetry readings and tax advice. I've never spent so much time

Despite the computer revolution, books promise to be vital for the foreseeable future.

in bookstores or bought so many books.'

So how is all this affecting the world of Christian books?

There is a huge amount of Christian material on the Internet, with churches, Christian organisations and individuals around the world all spreading their own news and views. But the potential of the Internet is being viewed more hesitantly by Christian publishers, as indeed with secular ones.

Some publishers have dipped a toe into electronic books. After all, the computer is ideal for encyclopaedias and cross-reference works. Bible students are already appreciating such works in multimedia formats, and books like the *Lion Handbook of the Bible* and various versions of the Bible are available on CD-ROM.

The Scripture Union has made a brave start by putting Bible reading notes onto the Web.

With all these developments, the still-unresolved problem is how to make it pay.

Who reads what?

Figures show that there are still as many Christian bookshops around – 578 in 1993, 579 in 1995. But sales of Christian books fluctuate. Sales for 1991 topped £50m. This had dropped by 20 per cent by 1993, followed in 1995 by a 26 per cent increase over the 1993 figure.

A survey published in 1996 conducted by Christian Research came up with some surprises. It's not only Christians in the pews who often don't read, many ministers and church leaders don't too.

It found that some ministers read nothing at all, while 36 per cent read 20 or more books a year. The average response was 15 books a year, of which eight are Christian and seven are general books.

Churchgoers read on average ten books a year, of which four are Christian and six general. They buy two Christian books a year (presumably borrowing the other two).

Surprisingly, just 43 per cent of ministers aged under 30 said they were expected to read as part of their work. A sixth of clergy, it seems, are effectively non book-readers.

Reading by example

Church leaders have a crucial role to play in encouraging the use of Christian literature. If they recognise the value of books in feeding their flock, it can influence the whole church. For reading Christians are growing Christians.

In the survey, 1 per cent of ministers said they recommended a book to their congregations every week, 12 per cent did so once a month, and 50 per cent did so two to three times a year. The average was three recommendations a year.

Paul Crockett of the Oxford bookshops says, 'The emphasis in the church makes a huge difference. It's not how the bookstall is run, more the leadership in the church which gets people to read. If leaders recognise the worth of books in their congregation's spiritual growth and continually put books before the people, it can influence the whole church.'

He finds that a lot of Christian books are bought for young children, up to the age of perhaps 7 or 8. Over that age, when they choose what they want to read, the problem is one of exposure.

'Parents have a tremendous influence on children's reading. It's up to the parents – if they have lots of books in the house and read a lot, it influences their children.

'One of the most important times for me is reading to each of my children each evening. It's the one time when each has me to themselves.'

Rita Harris, who has been involved in Gold Hill Church bookshop for 15 years, says, 'Book reading is going down even among church members. People buy books for little tots, then reading drops away. Parents are not reading, they are not encouraging their children to read. A few families are book mad but they're few and far between these days.'

Yet some say the tide is turning. Tony Bronnimann of the Maidenhead bookshop sees a distinct new trend towards books and Bible study among charismatic churches. Until now such churches have promoted reading far less than traditional evangelical churches.

Bishop David Pytches at Chorleywood certainly sees that happening: 'I think that reading Christian literature is probably increasing among Christians as more and more of them discover the benefits, enjoy the books and circulate them round. I certainly think that's what's happening here.'

Twelve of the most significant books in the history of St Andrew's Bookshop

J. I. Packer: *Knowing God*

Corrie ten Boom: *The Hiding Place*

David and Pat Alexander eds.: *Lion Handbook to the Bible*

David Wilkerson: *The Cross and the Switchblade*

Gerard Hughes: *God of Surprises*

Nicky Gumbel: *Questions of Life*

C. S. Lewis: *Mere Christianity*

John Stott: *Basic Christianity*

Steve Gaukroger: *It Makes Sense*

Adrian Plass: *The Sacred Diary of Adrian Plass Aged 37¾*

Joyce Huggett: *Listening to God*

Roy Hession: *Calvary Road*

Holme Grange Craft Village,
Wokingham

Holme Grange Craft Village,
Wokingham
RG40 3AW
Tel 01189 776715

Congratulations to St Andrew's Bookshops from all the team at Angus Hudson Ltd

Margaret and Ernie Barnett have always been special friends to the team at Angus Hudson Ltd. At every important moment, they have been there – for instance a landmark visit to the printer to celebrate the publishing of *The Lion Bible Handbook* – which we handled – they were there!

We shared in the trauma of the fire and the cost of replacing the losses. And St Andrew's have helped in building the Candle Books publishing list, experimenting with the Candle Booksellers Support Scheme and the excitement of installing the impressive Candle Books display in the St Andrew's chain of shops. As a team, we wish them well, and thank them for their wonderful friendship. We look forward to a future when Christians will continue to be committed to the ministry of Christian literature. *"Cooperation like that with Angus Hudson Ltd is typical of the cooperation St Andrew's Bookshop has enjoyed with all our suppliers, and has helped make this story come about." – Ernie Barnett*